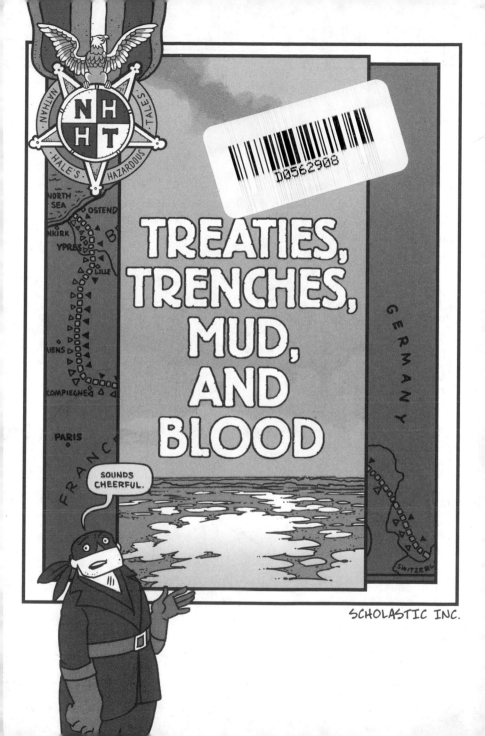

5

CHAPTER 1
THE ANCIENT MENAGERIE

OH JOY! IT'S LIKE A ZOO!

HERE IS EUROPE IN **1914.** EACH COUNTRY IS NOW REPRESENTED BY AN ANIMAL.

THESE ARE THE KEY PLAYERS IN **WORLD WAR ONE.** LET'S TAKE A LOOK AT EACH OF THEM.

YEAH! YEAH! YEAH!

LOOK! A MAGIC BIRD AND A *PUPPY!* THIS IS MY KIND OF STORY!

OOH! WHY ARE THEY SO **MAD** AT EACH OTHER?

THAT'S AUSTRIA-HUNGARY AND SERBIA-- AND THIS IS WHERE WE BEGIN.

THE AUSTRO-HUNGARIAN EMPIRE
REPRESENTED BY: THE *GRIFFIN*
(SYMBOL OF THE HOUSE OF HAPSBURG)

SERBIA IS A DANGEROUS *TROUBLEMAKER!* SOMEBODY NEEDS TO TEACH THAT COUNTRY A LESSON!

THE SOONER THE BETTER.

1914 POP. 50 MILLION
LEADER: EMPEROR FRANZ JOSEPH I
ALLIES: GERMANY

THE KINGDOM OF SERBIA
REPRESENTED BY: THE *WOLF*
(A NATIONAL ANIMAL OF SERBIA)

GIVE ME BACK MY FRIENDS, YOU WICKED OLD *BUZZARD!*

1914 POP. 4.5 MILLION
LEADER: KING PETER I, P.M. NIKOLA PAŠIĆ
ALLIES: RUSSIA

RUSSIA COULD **STEAMROLL** BOTH OF YOU!

THE GERMAN EMPIRE WOULD LIKE TO SEE THEM *TRY!*

WE ARE PREPARED FOR *ANYTHING!*

BUT WE ARE *BIGGER.*

YES, AND SLOWER!

EXCUSEZ-MOI, MESSIEURS, IF YOU MESS WITH RUSSIA, YOU ARE MESSING WITH *FRANCE!*

YOU!? WE DEFEATED YOU IN 1871!

YOU **STOLE OUR** LAND! ALSACE-LORRAINE IS **OURS!** GIVE US THE CHANCE-- WE'LL TAKE OUR LANDS AND OUR *REVENGE!*

THE **REPUBLIC OF FRANCE**
REPRESENTED BY: THE GALLIC ROOSTER

DON'T PUSH FRANCE. WE WILL PUSH BACK.

1914 POP. 35 MILLION
LEADER: PRÉSIDENT RAYMOND POINCARÉ
ALLIES: RUSSIA, ENGLAND

THE **KINGDOM OF BELGIUM**
REPRESENTED BY: THE **LION**
(BELGIUM'S NATIONAL ANIMAL)

WHY IS BELGIUM HERE? WE ARE A NEUTRAL COUNTRY! AND WE PLAN TO STAY NEUTRAL!

1914 POP. 7.6 MILLION
LEADER: KING ALBERT 1
ALLIES: *NEUTRAL*

10

12

13

WHAT ARE BELGIUM'S PLANS? YOU DIDN'T SHOW THEM.

YEAH! AND YOU FORGOT AMERICA TOO. I WANNA SEE THOSE BUNNIES!

BELGIUM IS NEUTRAL. THEIR PLAN IS TO STAY OUT OF WAR.

AND YET THEY GET TO BE THE *LIONS*...

AMERICA IS FAR FROM EUROPE, THEY HAVE NO REASON TO GET INVOLVED.

WONDER WHAT THEM COUNTRIES OVERSEAS IS UP TO.

DON'T RIGHTLY KNOW, DON'T RIGHTLY *CARE*.

NONE OF THIS IS ANYTHING NEW --EUROPE HAS ALWAYS BEEN AT WAR WITH ITSELF.

TRUE, BUT WEAPONS ARE BIGGER AND BADDER IN 1914. NEW TECHNOLOGY WILL LEAD TO A WHOLE NEW TYPE OF WAR.

WON'T THEY USE LANCES, GUNS, AND BAYONETS, LIKE ALWAYS?

THEY'LL USE ALL OF THOSE, SURE. BUT THE GUNS ARE BIGGER NOW.

1776 6-POUND HOWITZER

1914 14 cm RAIL GUN

WE HAVE ALSO ENTERED THE AGE OF THE *MACHINE GUN*.

WHAT'S A MACHINE GUN? IT LOOKS UGLY.

YOU'LL FIND OUT. AND IT *IS* UGLY.

IF YOUR NEIGHBOR IS STOCKPILING WEAPONS, WHAT DO YOU DO?

MOVE?

YOU BUILD AN ARSENAL YOURSELF!

THIS IS WHAT HAPPENS IN EUROPE. NO COUNTRY *WANTS* WAR--

I THINK GERMANY MIGHT WANT IT.

-- BUT EACH COUNTRY *PREPARES* FOR IT.

SENSIBLE. BETTER SAFE THAN SORRY.

BEFORE LONG, EVERYONE WILL BE **SORRY** AND NO ONE WILL BE SAFE.

15

17

18

19

20

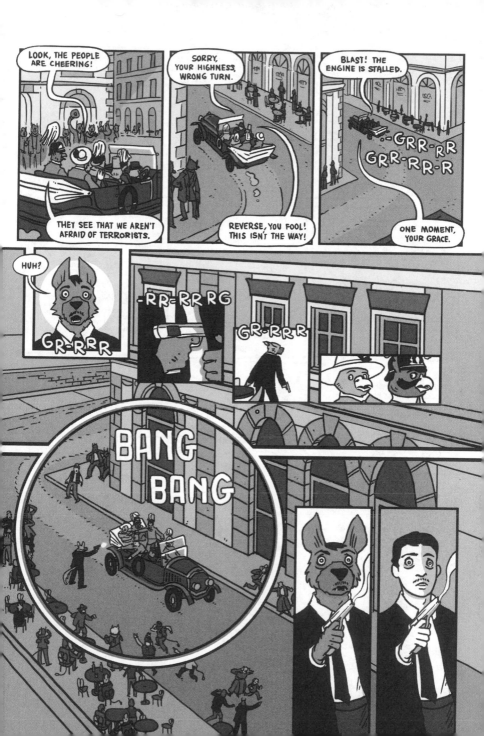

27

CHAPTER 6
THE KING OF THE BELGIANS
ROYAL PALACE BRUSSELS, BELGIUM

EVERYONE IS DECLARING WAR ON EACH OTHER. IT MAKES ME PROUD TO BE BELGIAN AND NEUTRAL.

BUT ALBERT, WHAT IF THE WAR SPILLS OVER OUR BORDERS? WHAT IF SOMEONE *INVADES*?

EVERYONE HAS SIGNED OUR NEUTRALITY AGREEMENT, THEY AREN'T *ALLOWED* TO INVADE.

KING ALBERT, YOUR MAJESTY, A MESSAGE FROM *GERMANY*:

AUGUST 2, 1914
TO THE BELGIAN MINISTER OF FOREIGN AFFAIRS,

WE HAVE RELIABLE INFORMATION THAT *FRANCE* IS PLANNING TO MARCH THROUGH BELGIUM IN ORDER TO INVADE GERMANY.

WE FEAR THAT BELGIUM WILL NOT BE ABLE TO REPEL A LARGE FRENCH INVASION FORCE.

THEREFORE, FOR YOUR PROTECTION AND OURS, WE REQUIRE YOUR PERMISSION TO ENTER BELGIUM.

THE SNEAKY DEVILS! THEY WANT TO SAVE US FROM *INVASION* BY *INVADING US!*

FRANCE IS OUR FRIEND, THEY WOULD *NEVER* INVADE US!

DOES GERMANY THINK WE'LL BELIEVE THIS? HOW STUPID DO THEY THINK WE ARE?

THEY PLAN TO INVADE FRANCE --AND I SUSPECT THEY WANT TO USE *US* AS THEIR INVASION ROUTE.

BUT WHY?

HOLLAND
BELGIUM
FRANCE
GERMANY
SWITZ.
ITALY

FRANCE'S BORDER IS *HEAVILY* DEFENDED. THEIR FORTRESSES FORM A STRONG BARRIER.

WE HAVE STRONG FORTRESSES TOO!

THAT'S WHY THE GERMANS ARE ASKING *NICELY.*

IF WE LET THEM MARCH THROUGH OUR BORDERS THEY WILL BYPASS *ALL* OF FRANCE'S DEFENSES.

WE'RE A *NATION*-- NOT A *ROAD!*

31

BELGIUM HAS GUARANTEED NEUTRALITY--AND WE'RE *BREAKING IT!*

ENGLAND WILL ATTACK US FOR THIS.

ENGLAND WILL ATTACK US ANYWAY.

FORWARD! THERE ISN'T A MINUTE TO LOSE!

I HAVE A PRECISE TIMETABLE! ONE MILLION TROOPS, ELEVEN THOUSAND TRAINS--ALL *TIMED PERFECTLY!*

BLOW UP ALL OF OUR BRIDGES ON THE GERMAN BORDER-- RAILROADS AND TUNNELS TOO!

SHOULD WE CALL FRANCE OR ENGLAND FOR HELP?

NOT JUST YET.

SURELY THE KAISER WILL COME TO HIS SENSES AND CALL OFF THIS *MAD* INVASION.

THE BRIDGE AT VISÉ, DESTROYED AUGUST 4, 1914

I LIKE THIS KING ALBERT. HE'S A BRAVE MAN IN A DIFFICULT POSITION.

I STILL THINK ENGLAND SHOULD BE THE LIONS.

BELGIUM *DESERVES* TO BE THE LIONS! THEY ARE ABOUT TO FIGHT THE GERMANS WITH A *CHOCOLATE ARMY!*

HANGMAN, I HATE TO DISAPPOINT YOU...BUT--

BUT WHAT? AWWWW. THEY AREN'T MADE OF CHOCOLATE, ARE THEY?

I THOUGHT THAT SOUNDED TOO GOOD TO BE TRUE.

34

35

38

39

40

43

44

46

CHAPTER 14 "PROTECT PARIS!"

ATTACK AND RETREAT!

ATTACK AND RETREAT!

CUT THESE TELEGRAPH WIRES.

BLOW UP THESE TRAIN TRACKS.

THIS IS MY HOMETOWN --WE USE THESE RAILROADS.

DO YOU WANT THE GERMANS TO HAVE THEM?

BLOW THEM UP!

THE MEN ARE EXHAUSTED. WE'VE BEEN MARCHING 25 MILES A DAY FOR THE PAST FOUR DAYS.

KEEP THEM MARCHING! WE ARE ALMOST TO PARIS!

MEANWHILE, IN PARIS...

WE SHOULD LEAVE!

THEY BURNED LOUVAIN--THEY'LL BURN PARIS, TOO!

CURSE ZOSE EAGLES! I HATE ZEM SO MUCH!

STOP SHOUTING AND START DIGGING! WE NEED TO BUILD DEFENSES!

I BROUGHT MY OWN SPADE.

WE'LL NEED 10,000 MORE JUST LIKE IT.

BARRICADE ALL ENTRANCES TO THE CITY-- EVEN THE SEWERS!

LET'S SEE ZOSE EAGLES GET THROUGH ZAT!

48

49

BY NOT HEADING STRAIGHT TO PARIS, THE GERMANS MADE A TACTICAL ERROR. THE FRENCH SPOTTED THE MISTAKE AND PREPARED TO **OUTFLANK** VON KLUCK'S ARMY.

WHAT DOES "OUTFLANK" MEAN?

HMMM. THINK OF THE GERMAN ARMY AS A BIG SNAKE.

CAN IT HAVE AN EAGLE HEAD?

ABSOLUTELY.

SUPPLIES MUNITIONS ENGINEERS FOOD MEDIC

THE MOST DANGEROUS PART OF AN ARMY IS THE FRONT--THE *HEAD*, THAT'S WHERE THE WEAPONS ARE.

SO YOU TRY TO ATTACK THE SNAKE FROM THE SIDE-- HIT THE **BODY** BEFORE THE HEAD CAN GET YOU!

SUPPLIES MUNITI

ALL OF THE SNAKES --I MEAN, *ARMIES*-- WERE LINED UP HEAD-TO-HEAD, READY TO CLASH.

THE FRENCH AND BRITISH ARMIES WERE CRAWLING BACKWARDS IN A TACTICAL RETREAT.

SEINE R.

MAUNOURY-SIXTH

PARIS

PARIS GARRISON

KLUCK

MOTTE

MARNE R.

BULOW

2ND

3RD

HAUSEN

NINTH-FOCH

FIFTH-FRA

4TH

FOURTH-LANGLE

ALBR

5TH

THIRD SA

THE BRITISH ARMY DOESN'T DESERVE THIS MONSTROSITY!

THE SPY PLANE SAW THAT VON KLUCK'S ARMY WAS TURNING.

SIXTH

KLUCK

1ST

AND THIS SNAKE COULD ATTACK ITS FLANK! BRILLIANT!

THIS OPENED A GAP FOR THE B.E.F. TO CHARGE INTO.

SIXTH

KLUCK

B.E.F.

FIFTH-FRANCH-D'ESPERE

2ND

SOON, THE GERMAN 1ST ARMY WAS IN TROUBLE.

50

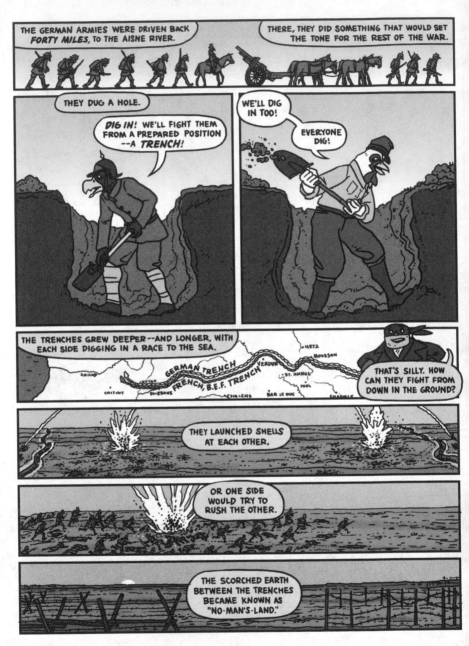

THE GERMAN ARMIES WERE DRIVEN BACK *FORTY MILES*, TO THE AISNE RIVER.

THERE, THEY DID SOMETHING THAT WOULD SET THE TONE FOR THE REST OF THE WAR.

THEY DUG A HOLE.

DIG IN! WE'LL FIGHT THEM FROM A PREPARED POSITION --A *TRENCH!*

WE'LL DIG IN TOO!

EVERYONE DIG!

THE TRENCHES GREW DEEPER --AND LONGER, WITH EACH SIDE DIGGING IN A RACE TO THE SEA.

GERMAN TRENCH
FRENCH, B.E.F. TRENCH

THAT'S SILLY. HOW CAN THEY FIGHT FROM DOWN IN THE GROUND?

THEY LAUNCHED SHELLS AT EACH OTHER,

OR ONE SIDE WOULD TRY TO RUSH THE OTHER.

THE SCORCHED EARTH BETWEEN THE TRENCHES BECAME KNOWN AS "NO-MAN'S-LAND."

PASSCHENDAELE

THE ORIGINAL B.E.F. WAS ALL BUT DESTROYED. BRITAIN WOULD HAVE TO REPLACE THESE SOLDIERS WITH RAW RECRUITS AND TERRITORIAL FORCES.

THIS STRETCH OF TRENCHES, KNOWN AS THE YPRES SALIENT, WOULD SEE MANY MORE BATTLES.

THE FIGHTING FROZE AS WINTER SETTLED IN.

BOTH SIDES DUG DEEPER INTO THEIR TRENCHES TO WAIT OUT THE COLD STANDSTILL.

POLYGON WOOD

BRITISH · KILLED, WOUNDED OR MISSING: 55,000

GERMAN · KILLED, WOUNDED OR MISSING: 134,000

58

60

75

THE BUNNIES

ON APRIL 6, 1917, SOMEBODY *NEW* JOINED THE WAR-- *THE AMERICANS.*

BUNNIES!

WHY THE CHANGE OF MIND NOW-- AFTER TWO AND A HALF *YEARS?*

WHEN THE *LUSITANIA* SANK, TEDDY ROOSEVELT, A FORMER U.S. PRESIDENT, SPOKE OUT FURIOUSLY AGAINST THE GERMANS.

THEY ARE NO BETTER THAN MURDERING **PIRATES**! WE SHOULD GO **TO WAR**!

WOODROW WILSON, THE CURRENT U.S. PRESIDENT, HAD OTHER PLANS.

THE UNITED STATES WILL **NOT** GO TO WAR.

AMERICAN AMMUNITION FACTORIES WERE SABOTAGED, BOMBS WERE PLANTED, A GERMAN SPY RING WAS CAPTURED -- STILL,

PRESIDENT WOODROW WILSON REMAINED FIRM.

WAR?

SPIES AMONG US?

BOMB SCARE!

"THERE WILL BE NO WAR. IT WOULD BE A CRIME AGAINST CIVILIZATION FOR US TO GO INTO IT."

THE AMERICAN PUBLIC HAD MIXED OPINIONS.

WE SHOULD GO FIGHT THOSE GERMANS!

I AM GERMAN!

I EMIGRATED TO AMERICA TO GET *AWAY* FROM THIS KIND OF TROUBLE.

I HOPE THEY FIGHT FOREVER. MY MUNITIONS FACTORY IS MAKING ME *MILLIONS!*

THE GERMANS EVEN SENT WORD THAT AMERICAN SHIPS WOULD BE TARGETED.

MR. PRESIDENT,

WE WILL SINK *ANY* SHIPS IN THE ALLIED WAR ZONE, NEUTRAL OR NOT.

THE GERMANS

THIS IS FOR SHOW.

THEY WON'T *REALLY* SINK OUR SHIPS.

THINK WE'RE BLUFFING?

JUST WATCH.

91

WHEN THE RAIN CLEARED, THE ALLIES PUSHED FORWARD.

LOOK AT THAT. IT'S GREEN OVER THERE.

I SEE ACTUAL TREES.

THE RAIN HAD GONE, BUT THE MUD REMAINED.

CAREFUL. DON'T FALL OFF THEM DUCKBOARDS, YOU WON'T CLIMB OUT OF THAT MUD.

IT AIN'T JUST MUD, EITHER.

RIFLES JAMMED, THEIR WORKINGS CLOGGED WITH MUD.

COMBAT WAS OFTEN HAND-TO-HAND.

ON NOVEMBER 6, THE CANADIANS TOOK PAASCHENDAELE.

IS THIS IT? IS THIS THE TOWN?

JUST LOOKS LIKE A PILE OF BRICKS.

NOW HOLD ON A MINUTE-- WHERE ARE THE *BUNNIES?*

PERSHING AND HIS FORWARD GROUP ARRIVED IN ENGLAND IN JUNE. THIS WAS THE FIRST TIME AN AMERICAN ARMY HAD EVER APPEARED IN ENGLAND.

THE KING OF ENGLAND MET WITH GENERAL PERSHING.

IT HAS ALWAYS BEEN MY DREAM THAT THE TWO ENGLISH-SPEAKING NATIONS SHOULD SOMEDAY BE UNITED IN A GREAT CAUSE.

AND TODAY, MY DREAM IS REALIZED!

THERE YOU HAVE IT. ALLIES AND FRIENDS.

WELL, I'LL BE.

96

98

CHAPTER 35

ASSEMBLY LINE

As the war grew and grew, so did the factories that made the war machines.

BIGGER GUNS! LONGER RANGE!

MORE SHELLS, MORE SHELLS!

BOMB THEIR FACTORIES! SEND OUT THE ZEPPELINS!

ZEPPELINS ARE AN EASY TARGET!

The Allied planes shoot down all our zeppelins-- they're just too *SLOW*.

THEN SEND *PLANES*-- DROP BOMBS FROM *PLANES*!

Germany began using a new weapon: the strategic bomber plane.

They bombed London again and again.

BOMBER PLANES-- WE CAN BUILD THOSE TOO!

TARGET FACTORIES-- BLAST THEM TO BITS!

The air war became as important as the battles on land and sea.

WE DON'T HAVE TIME TO COVER THE FLYING ACES OF WWI--THEIR ADVENTURES DESERVE A FULL BOOK.

AWW.

99

108

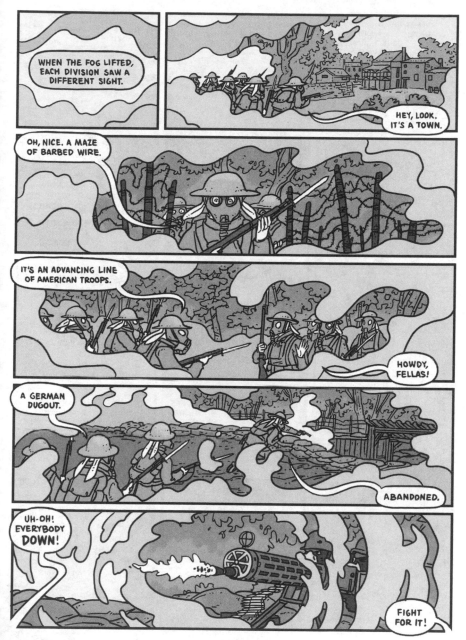

111

112

TWO HUNDRED SOLDIERS FROM THE 114TH DIVISION, NEW JERSEY, WENT INTO THE RAVINE.

THIRTEEN CAME OUT.

ANOTHER GROUP, THE 77TH *"STATUE OF LIBERTY"* DIVISION, WENT TOO FAR ALTOGETHER.

WHERE IS EVERYONE?

SEND OUT PATROLS-- CHECK WITH OUR SUPPORT DIVISIONS ON EITHER SIDE.

PATROLS ARE BACK. WE HAVE NO SUPPORT ON EITHER SIDE.

IN FACT, WE'RE SURROUNDED BY GERMANS.

HOLD TIGHT AND DIG IN.

WE'LL FIGHT 'EM OFF UNTIL OUR SUPPORT TROOPS *DO* ARRIVE.

INCOMING!

THOSE AREN'T GERMAN SHELLS! THOSE ARE *OURS*!

WE'RE BEING SHELLED BY OUR OWN GUYS!

113

114

115

117

124

BIBLIOGRAPHY

THE FIRST WORLD WAR:
A VERY SHORT INTRODUCTION
MICHAEL HOWARD
OXFORD UNIVERSITY PRESS, 2002

A WORLD UNDONE:
THE STORY OF THE GREAT WAR
G.J. MEYER
BANTAM DELL, 2006

THE GUNS OF AUGUST
BARBARA W. TUCHMAN
RANDOM HOUSE, 1962

TO CONQUER HELL:
THE MEUSE-ARGONNE, 1918
EDWARD G. LENGEL
HENRY HOLT AND COMPANY, 2008

LOST BATTALIONS:
THE GREAT WAR AND THE CRISIS
OF AMERICAN NATIONALITY
RICHARD SLOTKIN
HENRY HOLT AND COMPANY, 2005

A STORM IN FLANDERS:
THE YPRES SALIENT, 1914-1918
WINSTON GROOM
ATLANTIC MONTHLY PRESS, 2002

WORLD WAR I IN CARTOONS
MARK BRYANT
GRUB STREET PUBLISHING, 2006

AN ILLUSTRATED ENCYCLOPEDIA OF
UNIFORMS OF WORLD WAR I
JONATHAN NORTH AND JEREMY BLACK
ANNESS PUBLISHING, 2012

AN ILLUSTRATED HISTORY OF
THE FIRST WORLD WAR
JOHN KEEGAN
KNOPF, 2001

THE WAR TO END ALL WARS:
WORLD WAR I
RUSSELL FREEDMAN
CLARION BOOKS, 2010

THE GREAT WAR
26-EPISODE DOCUMENTARY
BBC, 1964

IT WAS THE WAR OF THE TRENCHES
JACQUES TARDI
FANTAGRAPHICS, 2010

GODDAMN THIS WAR!
JACQUES TARDI, JEAN-PIERRE VERNEY
FANTAGRAPHICS, 2013

BOOKS

BOOKS WITH LOTS OF PICTURES

VIDEO

COMICS (NOT KID FRIENDLY)

TO MY FIRST WORLD WAR I TEACHER, SNOOPY

ISBN 978-1-338-17981-1

12 11 10 9 8 7 6 5   19 20 21 22

Printed in the U.S.A.   23

First Scholastic printing, January 2017

Book design by Nathan Hale and Chad W. Beckerman